HOW TO USE THE STENCILS

1. WASH THE PUMPKIN OR WIPE IT WITH A DAMP CLOTH TO REMOVE ANY DUST AND DIRT. LET IT AIR DRY, OR USE A PAPER TOWEL TO DRY IT COMPLETELY. IF YOU ARE CARVING THE PUMPKIN, THOROUGHLY CLEAN OUT THE INSIDE.

2. CHOOSE A PATTERN AND CAREFULLY CUT OUT THE SHEET FROM A BOOK

3. CUT OUT COARSELY AROUND THE PATTERN.

4. STICK THE TEMPLATE TO THE PUMPKIN WITH TAPE. USE A PENCIL TO MARK CLOSELY SPACED HOLES ALONG THE STENCIL LINES, PIERCING THE PAPER.

5. CAREFULLY CUT OUT ANY PREVIOUSLY TRACED LINES USING A KNIFE OR A SPECIAL PUMPKIN CARVING BLADE.

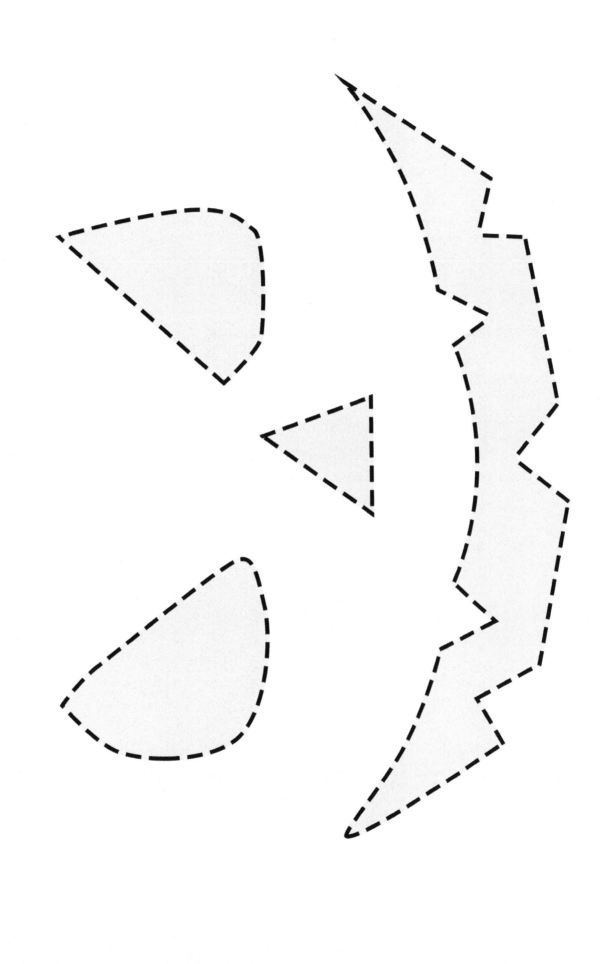

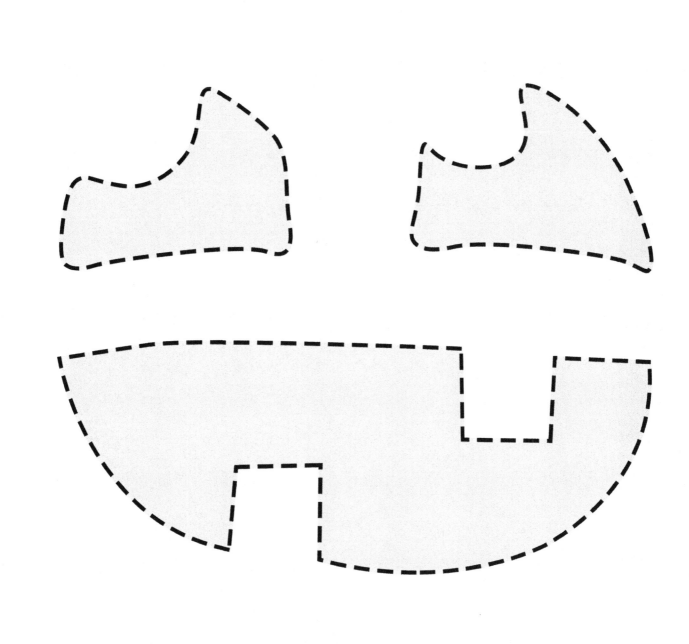

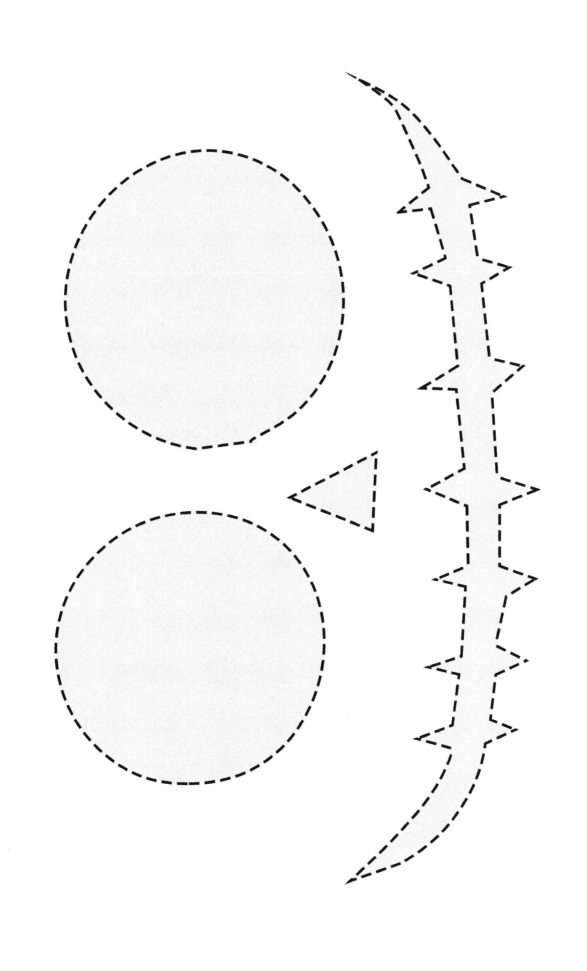

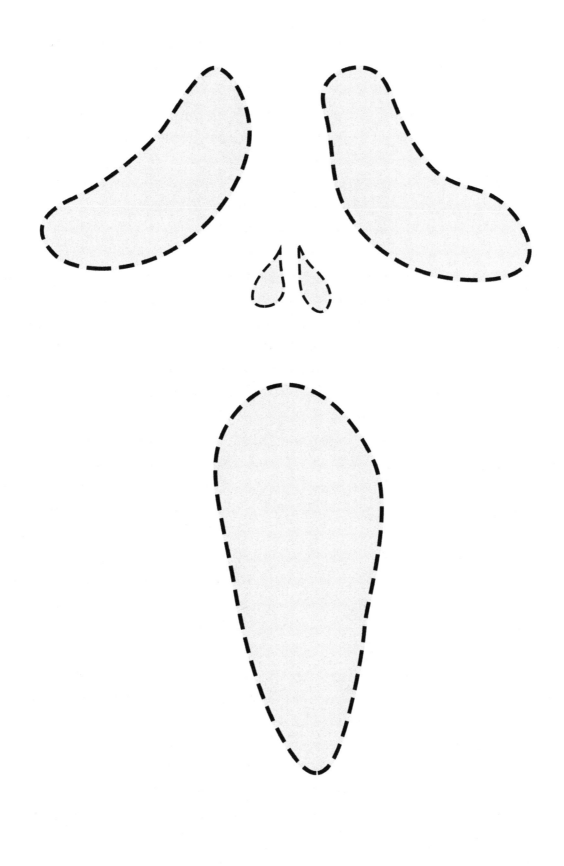

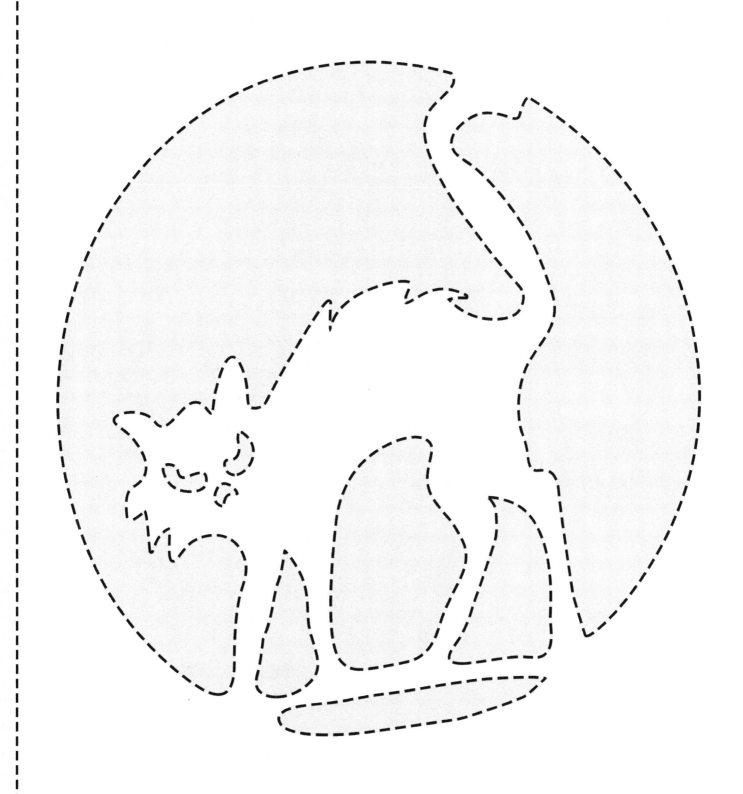

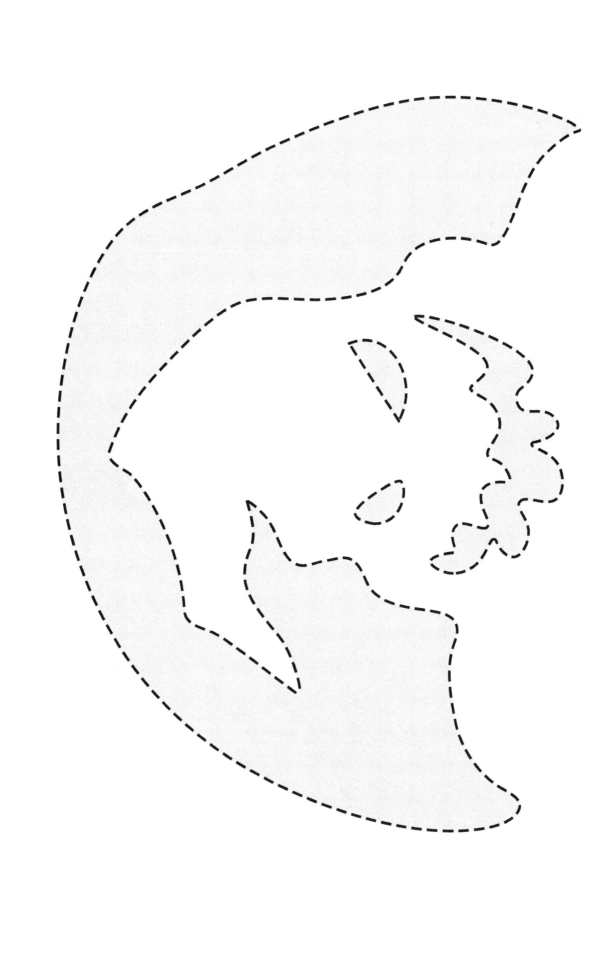

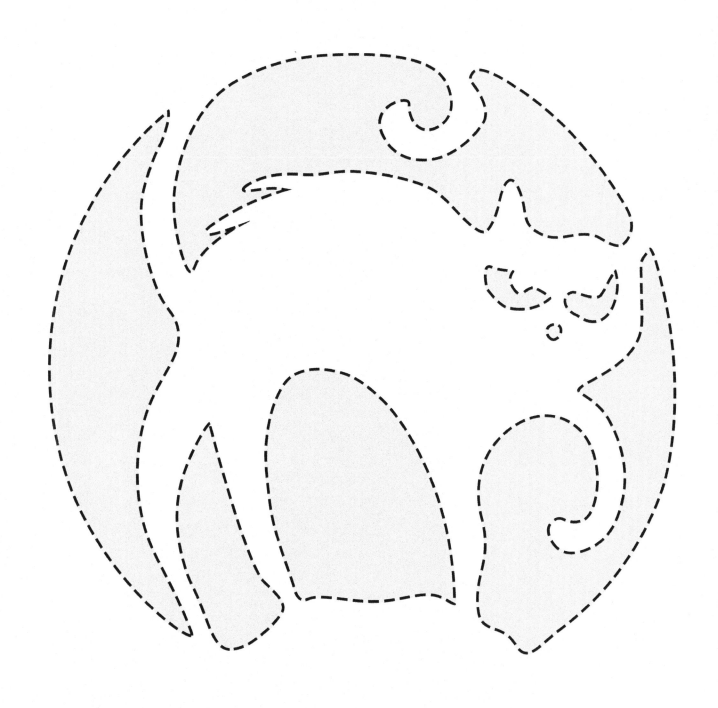

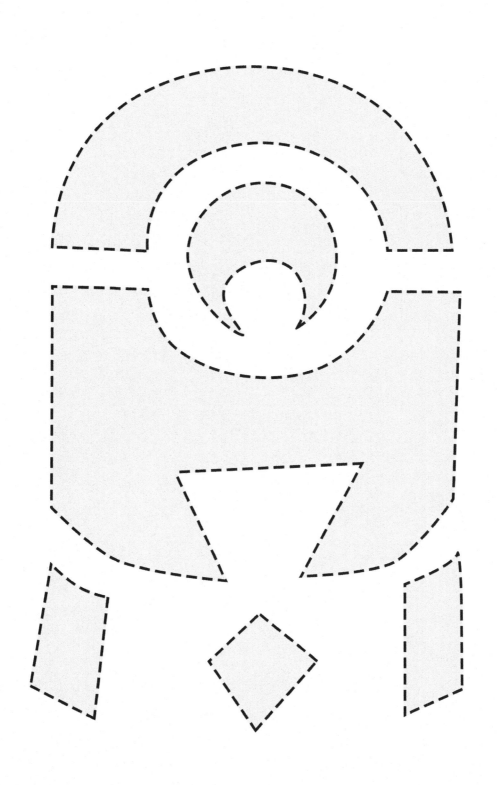

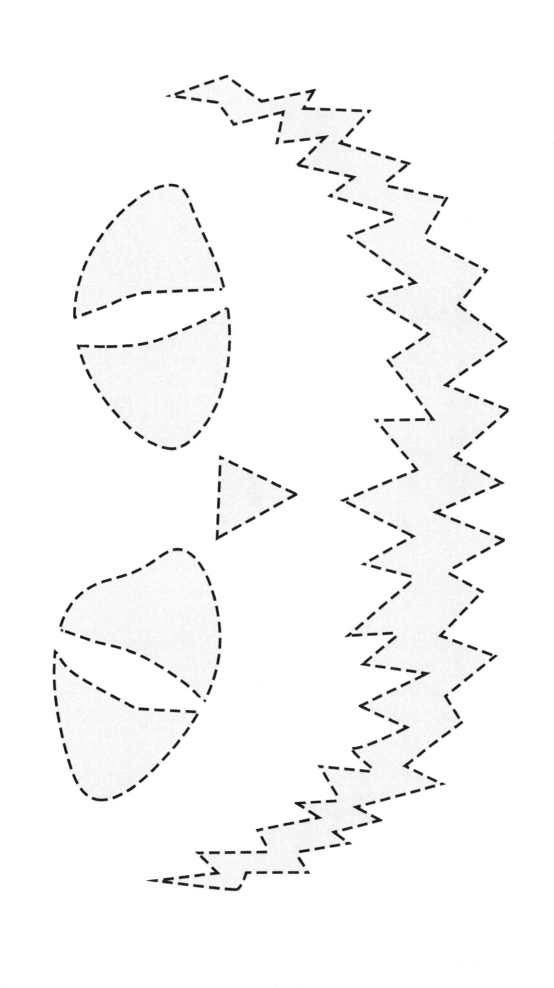

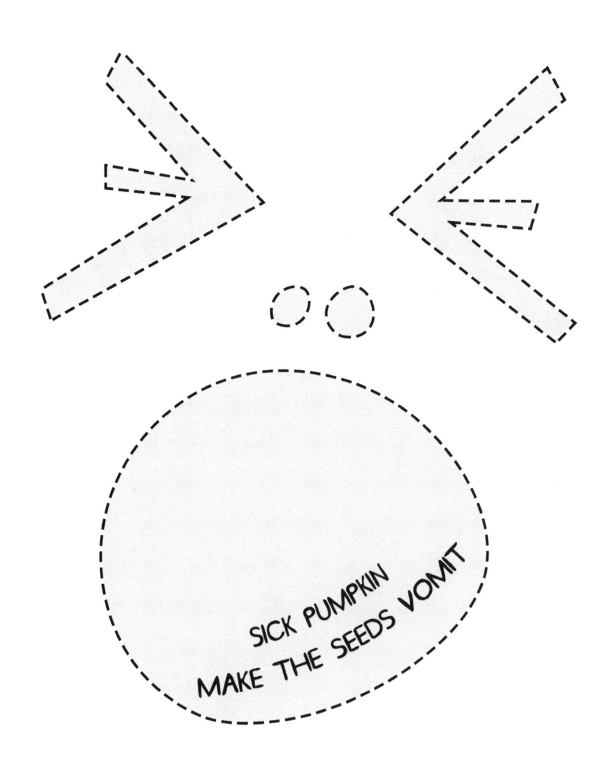

SICK PUMPKIN
MAKE THE SEEDS VOMIT

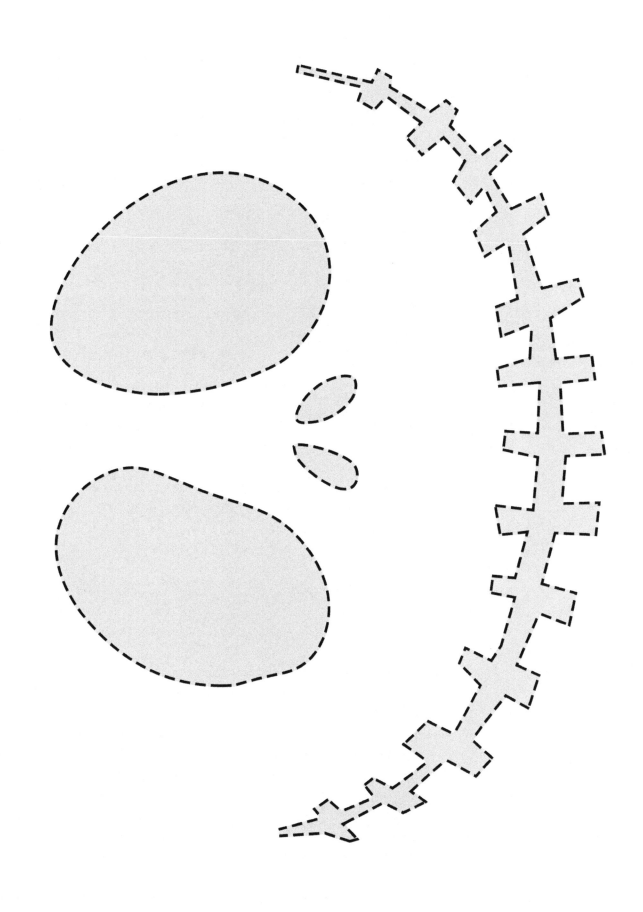

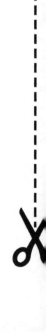

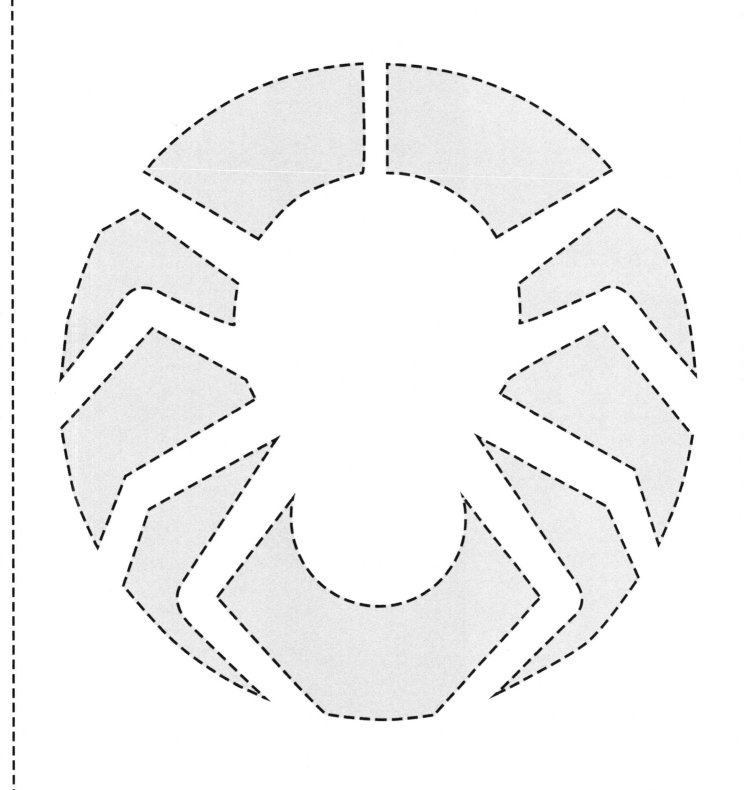

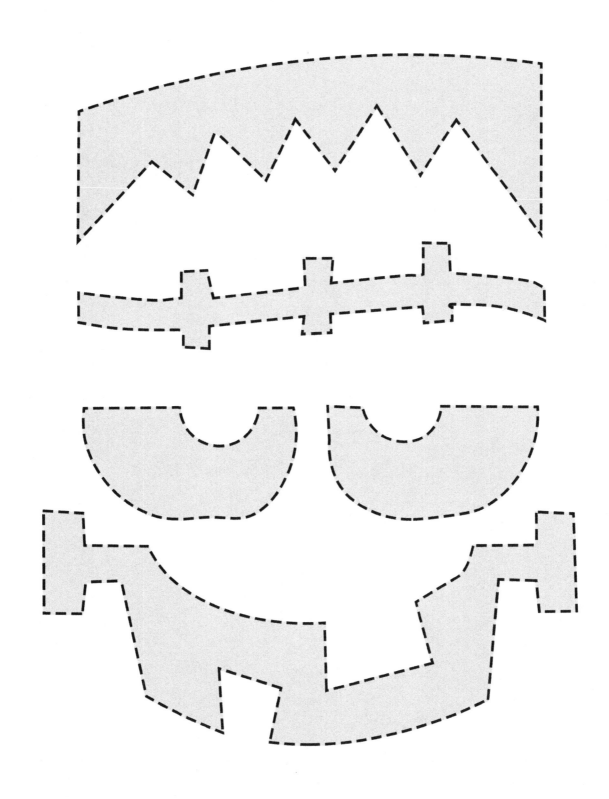

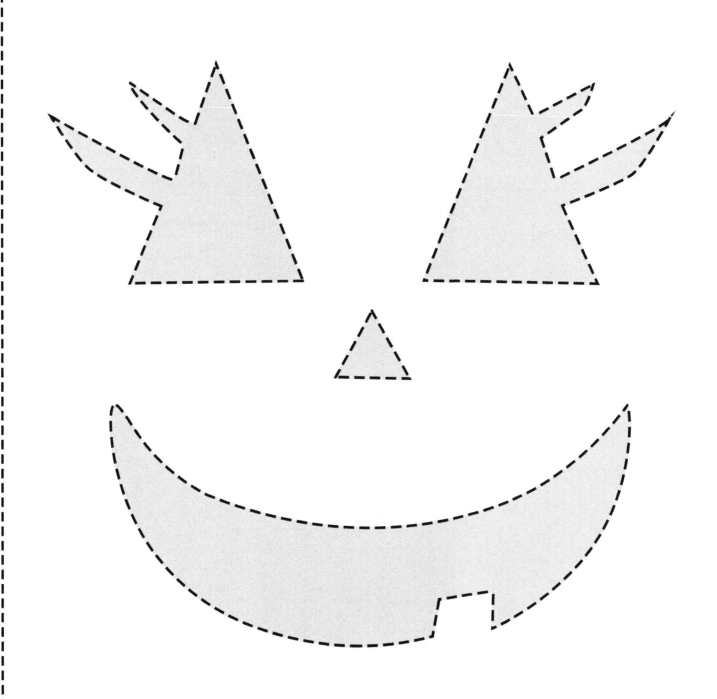

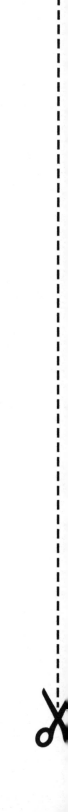

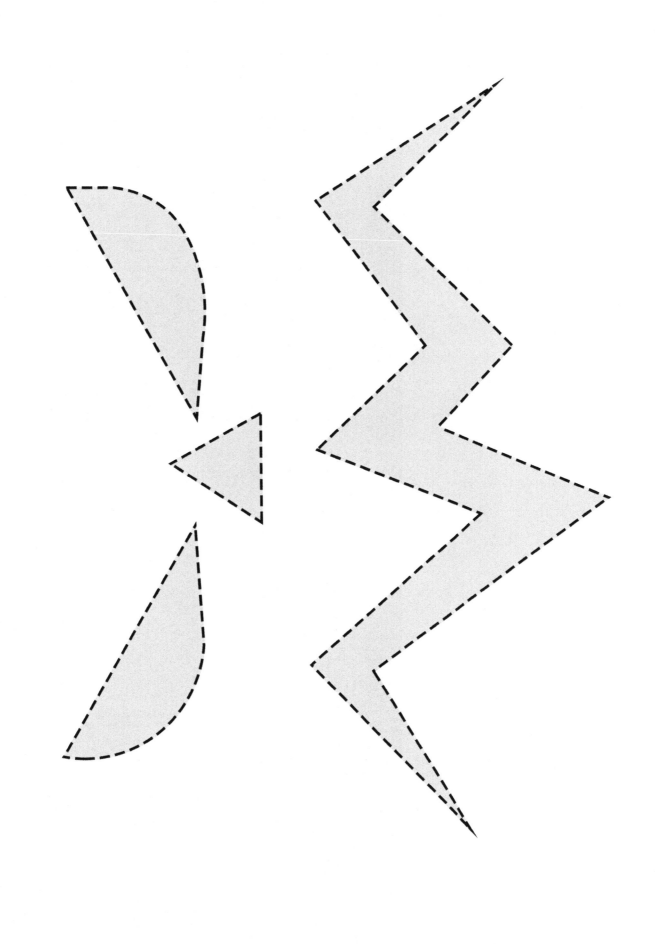

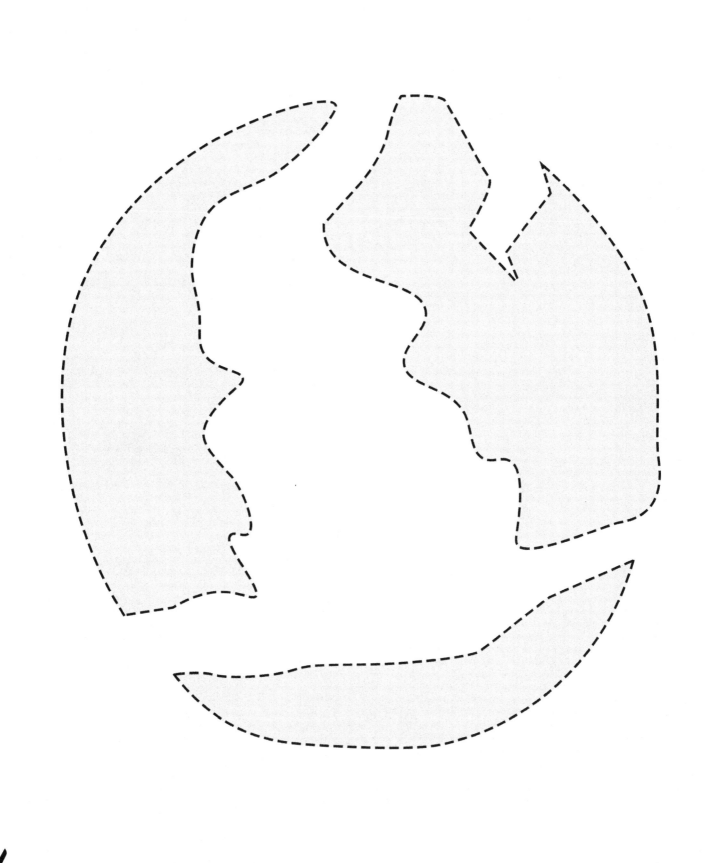

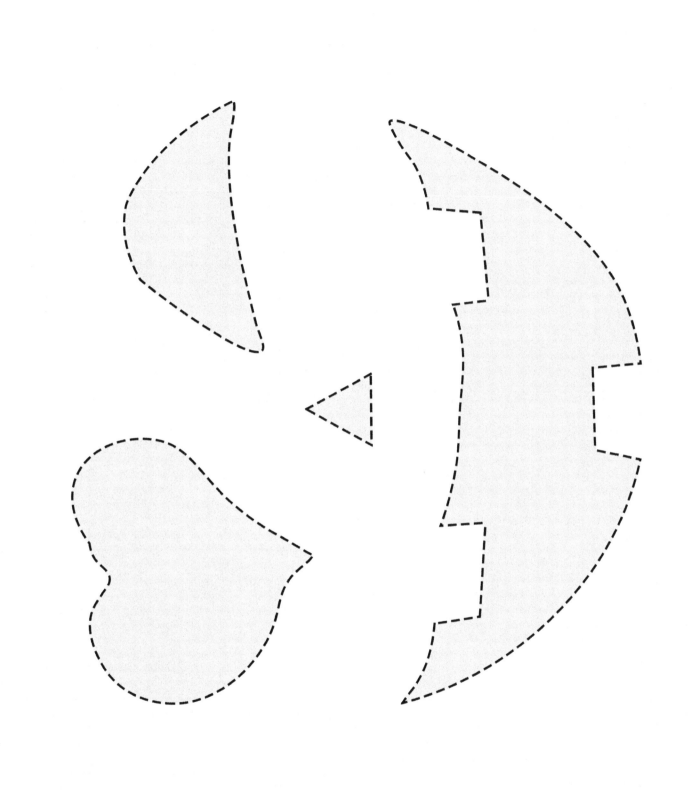